FAITH'S WORK PERFECTED.

The Orphan House at Halle.

II.

L. Renner sc. N. Afinger sc.

Inner view.

The Orphan House at Halle.

II.

Inner view.

FAITH'S WORK PERFECTED;

OR,

FRANCKE'S ORPHAN HOUSE AT HALLE.

By A. H. FRANCKE,

PROFESSOR IN THE HALLE UNIVERSITY, AND FOUNDER OF THE ORPHAN HOUSE.

EDITED AND TRANSLATED BY

WM. L. GAGE.

NEW YORK:

ANSON D. F. RANDOLPH,

770, BROADWAY, CORNER OF NINTH STREET.

MDCCCLXVII.

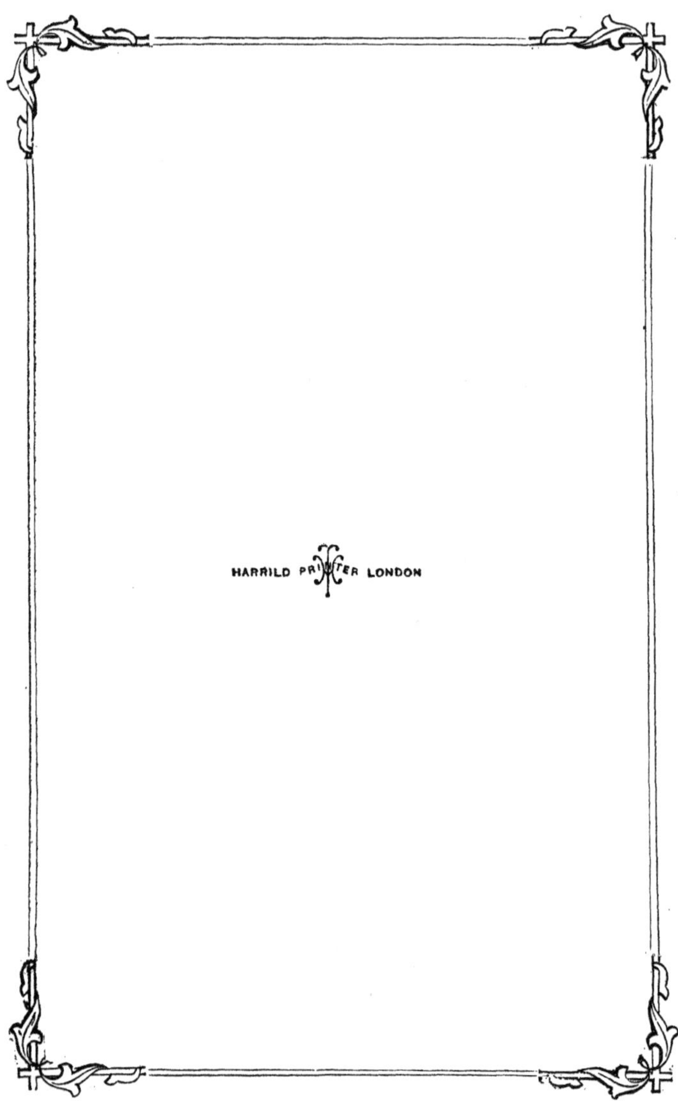

HARRILD PRINTER LONDON

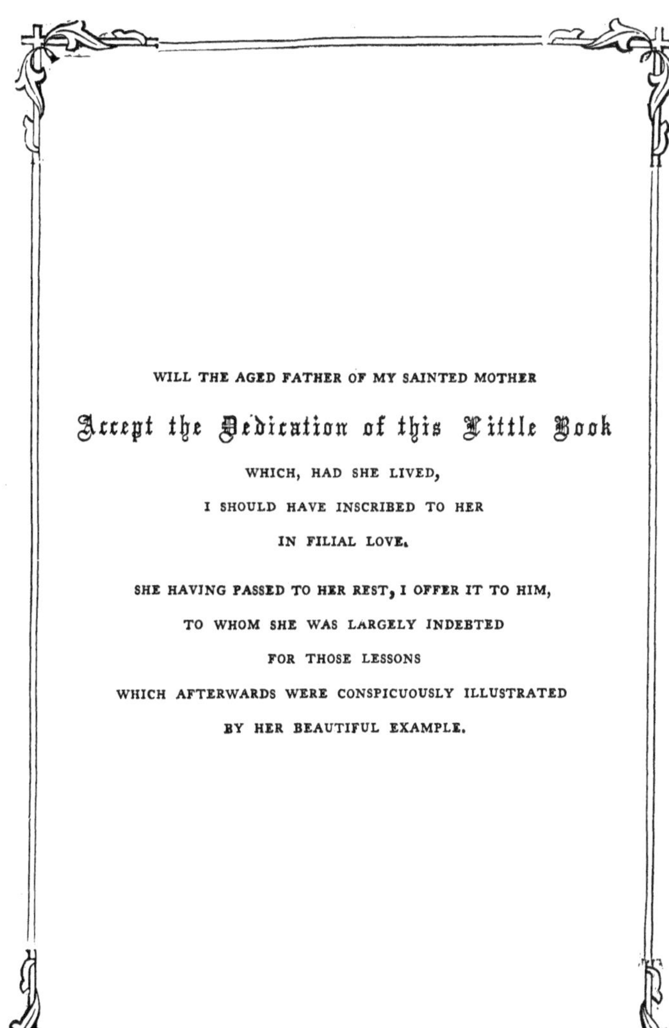

WILL THE AGED FATHER OF MY SAINTED MOTHER

Accept the Dedication of this Little Book

WHICH, HAD SHE LIVED,

I SHOULD HAVE INSCRIBED TO HER

IN FILIAL LOVE.

SHE HAVING PASSED TO HER REST, I OFFER IT TO HIM,

TO WHOM SHE WAS LARGELY INDEBTED

FOR THOSE LESSONS

WHICH AFTERWARDS WERE CONSPICUOUSLY ILLUSTRATED

BY HER BEAUTIFUL EXAMPLE.

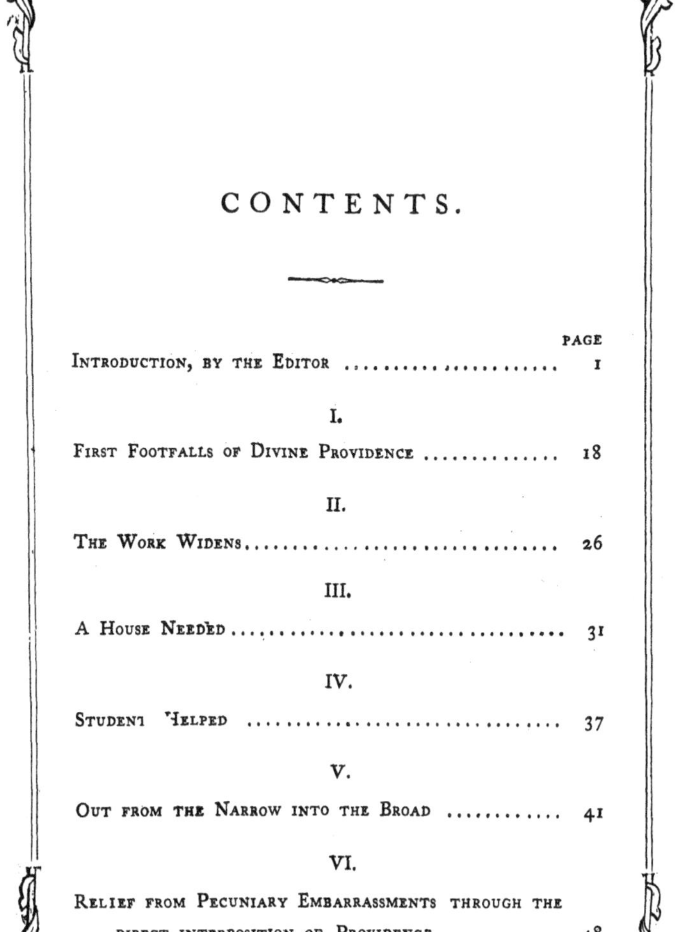

CONTENTS.

FAITH'S WORK PERFECTED;

OR,

FRANCKE'S ORPHAN HOUSE AT HALLE.

EDITOR'S INTRODUCTION.

NO visitor stops at the city of Halle in Germany in order to take the great theologian Tholuck by the hand, or to look at him with more timid respect in the lecture-room, without halting in one of the large public squares, and wondering what is the use of an immense yet not tasteless pile of buildings, which cluster there, and form one of the chief architectural features of the city. In palatial importance they entirely eclipse the University of Halle, spacious as even that is; and no hotel, no private mansion, not even that in which Napoleon took up his residence while he held the place, can be compared with it for a moment. This congeries of buildings occupies an entire square, and it is a good walk to compass it. I passed unchallenged up the staircase leading to the main entrance; thence through the lofty hall, with a bookseller's shop on the one side, and a drug shop on the other, into the spacious rectangle enclosed by buildings on all sides, and looked around me, endeavouring to conjecture the uses of the place. That instant an unseen bell struck; presently the square filled with such thronging multitudes of boys and girls, that it was plainly a school or a system of schools. Soon a young, intelligent-faced man walked by; him I accosted, and learned that I was standing within the world-renowned precincts of Francke's Orphan House.

A few days later a friend took me to a little bookstall in a retired street—so retired, that I wondered how any one ever found it out; in fact, not even a bookstall, but a lodging-room, where a Mr. Petersen, student of divinity, kept a meagre assortment of books, old and new, and now and then, through the kindness of friends, found a purchaser. This Mr. Petersen presently showed me a thick, square, worn book, very old and dingy, leather bound, coarsely printed, and wholly unattractive. He assured me that its contents were valuable—that it contained Francke's own account of the founding of the Orphan House, from the very inception to the perfect completion—with a valuable mass of appendices and original documents, throwing light upon the whole of that most remarkable history of the Triumph of Faith. For the trifling sum of fifty cents I became the possessor of this rare volume, whose worth I then only partly knew.

The next day as I was walking with Professor Tholuck, he remarked, "Before you leave Halle, you must, if possible, possess yourself of a curiosity." I inquired what it might be. "At the bookstall of Mr. Petersen, number so and so, in such and such a street," he went on to say, "you will find a book entirely out of print, and very rarely met; the entire history, from Francke's own hand, of the development of this great Orphan House of Halle. The price is only twenty silver groschen." I looked at him in amazement. How, thought I, do you know this? you, one of the most eminent of theologians, familiar with the contents of a little, retired bookstall? Of course I was not slow to answer that only the day before, I had found the book and become its possessor.

That book, bearing the curiously quaint title

THE MOST BLESSED FOOTSTEPS
OF THE LIVING AND REIGNING,
THE LOVING AND FAITHFUL GOD
FOR THE SHAMING OF THE UNBELIEVING,
AND THE STRENGTHENING OF THE BELIEVING,
DISCLOSED THROUGH THE TRUE AND CIRCUMSTANTIAL
HISTORY OF THE
ORPHAN HOUSE IN HALLE,

I have carefully perused and collated, drawing out and combining all that illustrates the great doctrines of faith and answered prayer. Much of it is now but cumbrous detail; the local regulations of the school, the lists of books, the catalogue raisonné of donations, the minute working of all the parts, were not to my purpose, and I have not used them, excepting in selections which seemed to illustrate the theme. The "Footsteps," the first of the bundle of pamphlets, I have retained in full. It was translated into Dutch and English about 1705, but it would probably be a hopeless task to try to resuscitate a quaint English version: the work is better done afresh. Of the continuations to the "Footsteps" I have made a careful use, and have tried to incorporate such of them as are pertinent.

There are two points of significance in the work of Francke, to which special attention ought to be called. One is the great ability, learning, and scope of the man. In this respect he seems to stand above any other one whose career has been familiar to the world as exhibiting an equally trusting faith in the living God. George Müller, while a man of powerfully organizing mind, is not known to the scholarly world as a lettered man, and never puts forth any effort to conciliate and convince the unbelief of men of nice and dainty culture. He has the simplicity of a child, but it is in his faith alone that he is most great, daring, and strong. His efficiency is that of prayer, enjoined with those humble qualities which, our Saviour assures us, are to inherit the kingdom of God. Heinrich Stilling, the well-known German mystic, whose autobiography was much read years ago, was able, by his downright honesty, his transparent purity, and his rare unworldliness, to win even Goethe as a friend; but I have long thought that Goethe was drawn to him as a study, as representing one phase of life, as the typical Pietist, rather than out of any deep sympathy or thorough appreciation of the man. And there is in Stilling such a romantic love of the marvellous, such a preference of it to any other thing, and so many whimsical vagaries (not all fully unfolded in his "Autobiography," but hinted at), that many would not be led to confess the power of prayer after reading that quaint, simple, and richly affectionate book with its wealth of faith and domestic love; who would perhaps be hindered rather than helped. So Huntingdon, author of the "Bank of Faith," has so much egotism, so many foolish conceits (witness, for illustration, his habit of appending S. S. to his name on the title-page of his book and on all occasions, which the reader learns at last, signifies Sinner Saved), that one wearies of his ignorance and of his diffuseness. True, the essence of good is there; the Christian can read that book and draw strength from it, but the man of the world, I have thought, might only be hardened by it.

But Francke is an entirely different type of man. He stands out as notable in his age as Dante does in his. He was a profound scholar, an eloquent preacher, a correct thinker, and a man of wonderful energy and organizing power. With Spener he founded the order of Pietists, and in an age when a subtle infidelity on the one side, and a dead traditional and entirely respectable religious formality on the other, were robbing

Germany of all deep and quick religious life, he was one of the very few, who preserved the sacred fire. Spener and Francke and Freling-huysen, the poet, are a trio whose Christian services to their age cannot be overrated. Any one who reads the admirable resumé of Francke's life which is contained in Herzog's invaluable "Encyclopædia," will discover that great as was the founding of the Orphan House, it was but a fragment of his life work. And in going over the "Footsteps" the reader will not discern one trait of weakness; the style is simple and direct, but utterly free from conceit and folly. Francke wins upon the reader as a wise and energetic man: wonderfully supported by his faith, wonderfully answered in his prayer, but uniting the child-like soul with a large power of influencing men, a comprehensive insight into character, and great sagacity and scope of understanding. Carlyle has caricatured him in his ribald, zig-zag way ("History of Frederick the Great," vol. ii. p. 18), and multitudes have accepted the lightning-like sketch as a faithful portrait.

"Did English readers," writes this remorseless pen, "ever hear of Francke? Let them make a momentary acquaintance with this famous German saint. August Hermann Francke, a Lübeck man, born 1663; Professor of Theology, of Hebrew, Lecturer on the Bible; a wandering, persecuted, pious man; founder of the 'Pietists,' a kind of German Methodists, who are still a famed sect in that country; and of the Waisenhaus at Halle, grand Orphan House, built by charitable beggings of Francke, which also still subsists; a reverend gentleman, very mournful of visage, now sixty-four, and for the present at Berlin, discoursing of things eternal in what Wilhelmina thinks a very lugubrious manner. Well, but surely in a very serious manner! The shadows of death were already round this poor Francke, and in a few weeks more he had himself departed. But hear Wilhelmina, what account she gives of his own and the young Grenadier Major's behaviour on these mournful occasions. The King had fallen into one of his hypochondrias, and had Francke, the Halle

Methodist, giving ghostly counsel; his Majesty ceased to have the newspapers read at dinner, and listened to lugubrious Francke's exhortations instead. Hear Wilhelmina—

"'His Majesty began to become valetudinary, and the hypochondria which tormented him rendered his humour very melancholy. Monsieur Francke, the famous Pietist, founder of the Orphan House at Halle University, contributed not a little to exaggerate that latter evil. This reverend gentleman entertained the King by raising scruples of conscience about the most innocent matters. He condemned all pleasures; damnable all of them, he said, even hunting and music. You were to speak of nothing but the Word of God only; all other conversation was forbidden. It was always he that carried on the improving talk at table, where he did the office of reader, as if it had been a refectory of monks. The King had us treated to a sermon every afternoon; his valet-de-chambre gave out a psalm, which we all sang. In a word, this dog of a Francke (ce chien de Francke) led us all the life of a set of monks of la Trappe.'"

The reader may give what credence he will to this account. I find no further proof of its accuracy than what every giddy, frivolous girl like Wilhelmina finds harsh and hard in a sedate, elderly clergyman, and what the virulent Carlyle finds in almost every Christian. Francke was an earnest, serious man, looking at life as a weighty thing—cheerful, hopeful, and happy; nowhere showing a sour or morbid spirit, and looked up to by even his opponents as a man of great talents, and a pillar in the land.

Another point is the magnitude of the work which he accomplished. I speak now of the Orphan House; but that was enough for any man's monument. With a capital of only three dollars and a half, and trusting in the living God's willingness to answer the prayer of faith, and believing in the FACT that He does answer the prayer of faith, he dared to begin that great undertaking, and was safely carried through it, and in a very few years saw it the foremost educational institution in Germany, and the most extensive eleemosynary asylum in the world. Before his death he witnessed over two thousand children sheltered at once within its walls, and all its departments—the Orphans' Home, the Theological Seminary, the Normal School, the Publishing, the Bookselling, and the Apothecaries' Departments, the Library, the Establishment for Widows, poor Students in the University, the Poor of the suburbs of Halle, and for strolling Beggars—in full and successful operation. It has changed but little from that time to this. The ample funds in possession of which he was able to leave the Orphan House have still increased, and when I was in Halle there were nearly four thousand children taught there; a corps of almost two hundred teachers were maintained, many living within the building; while the various appointments, the dining-rooms and reading-rooms, the school-rooms, hospital, and library, the offices and gymnasium, were all that were needed for the accommodation of such a host.

I will not go here into any recital of the history

of the institution—this Professor Francke has fully done in the "Footsteps." He takes the reader from the first stage, when money was counted in pence and halfpence, up to the last, when the House was in the receipt of a princely sum every year, twenty thousand dollars (gold) coming in from a single source. Carlyle has said this was the result of "charitable beggings." It was not. Francke appealed to no man for money. The King of Prussia did, indeed, after the institution was recognized as a power, grant a license to take collections for it in the parish churches of the kingdom; but the cost and the trouble were so great that it was soon abandoned, and indirectly led to pecuniary loss rather than gain. The book is an effective illustration of the truth that we *live* and *move*, as well as have our being, in God; that He is a *living* God, the prompter of every holy work; that his Spirit does indeed work within us, to will and to do after his good pleasure. Francke relied implicitly upon such a God. He believed so profoundly in Him that his belief became act. He knew that the Spirit of God was equal to the work which he wished to see done, and he was not disappointed. He did not sit down with folded hands, expecting to see a fair and stately building, fitly appointed, spring into being before his eyes. He worked incessantly, he planned, he brought men together, he assigned them their task; *then* he prayed. He asked the living God to move the hearts of his children to give according to their means for an object whose end was the glory of Christ. Had God left Himself without a witness, this prayer had been in vain; had there not been the Spirit of Christ in the people's hearts, only needing quickening and direction, this prayer had been in vain. But the "seed of the kingdom" was yet in the land. Infidelity and spiritual deadness had not buried it so deep but it might sprout yet, and bear fruit to the glory of God.

It is, of course, an open question, whether, in all the minute details of life, God *palpably* leads us, and *always* shows us the reason why He leads us as He does; and I think there is no advantage gained to Christianity in commenting on unanswered prayer with too close an appearance of intimacy with the Divine counsels respecting our lives. The faith of some may be strengthened, but the unbelief of others may be hardened by it. But in such a work as this, as well as in that part of George Müller's life which relates to his career as pastor in Teignmouth and Bristol, there is the evident work of the Spirit of God on the hearts of men, manifested in that normal method of diffusive beneficence which only seeks a worthy Christian object on which to bestow its gifts. The hearts of German Christians a hundred and sixty years ago had the same love of Christ which animates those who live to-day; and it only needed to be kindled by the power of Francke's life and preaching to prompt to giving even without direct appeal. There is surely no need of mysticism in this. It is one of the most open manifestations of the genuine Christian life. And Francke has painted it, not in glowing colours, but in an even-tempered tone, warm and devout, indeed, as he could only be, but dispassionate, calm, and overflowing with good sense and wise discrimination.

An interesting fact connected with Francke, is that by the law of spiritual genealogy, he was probably the religious father of George Müller. It is interesting to think that in Halle, Müller must have known much of the career of Francke. He carried his recollections to England, and in due time he too, in much the same way as the German of 1700, began *his* Orphan House. Thus do good men span the centuries; thus being dead, they yet speak; though they rest from their labours, their works do follow them. It seems a little thing to the readers of George Müller's life, that in his early manhood he made that sojourn in Halle during his wanderings; but it was the means, doubtless, of giving the great Bristol Asylum to the world.

It is a great pleasure to introduce so sound and healthful a book to the world. It has lain locked up in an obscure and difficult tongue for more than a century and a half, and yet it contains the eternal, indestructible truth of Christ.

To cull out this little faggot, I have had to turn over more than a thousand pages, yet the author's kindling fervour has made it a pleasant task, even when I have thought the words not concentrated enough for translation and publication. The gleaning of what is given here has been a delightful task to beguile the weary hours of a sick-room away; and it has been not the least among numberless mercies, that, while cut off from wonted activities by an invalid's lot, I could still speak from my chamber to the world.

W. L. GAGE.

I.

FIRST FOOTFALLS OF DIVINE PROVIDENCE.

IT was formerly the custom in the city of Halle and its environs, for the people to appoint a certain day on which the poor were allowed to assemble at their doors, and beg once a week for alms. In Glaucha, the little village where I lived, just on the outskirts of Halle, Thursday was the day on which they came to my door to receive their weekly allowance. I used for a long time to distribute bread to them in front of the house; but I thought afterwards that it would afford an excellent opportunity for me to reach their souls with some religious instruction, for the most of them were grossly ignorant, and many were even vicious.

So one day, as they stood in front of the house, I asked them all to come in; I arranged the older people on one side, and the younger on another, and began in a friendly way to ask the children some questions out of Luther's catechism, to see how much they knew about religion. Only the men and women listened; I did not spend more than a quarter of an hour or so in the catechizing, and closed with a prayer, then giving them their usual gifts, and telling them that in future I should try to provide something for both body and soul, and asking them to come to my house every Thursday in the same way, which they did. This was in the beginning of 1694.

When I discovered the excessive ignorance of these poor people, and found it hard to get an entering wedge to their minds, for the first principles of Christianity, I was for a long time very much troubled to know how I could make any impression upon them. It seemed a great shame to the Christian name that so many people should grow up like cattle, without any knowledge of divine things, and especially that so many children, in consequence of the poverty of their parents, should neither be sent to school, nor enjoy good training at home, but grow up in the most scandalous ignorance and vice, and when they arrived at mature years be fit for nothing, and know nothing but how to rob and steal, and commit every vice.

The attempt to send children to school, giving them the money to pay their weekly tuition, did not succeed; for it was found that they asked for the money indeed, but they either did not go to school at all, or if they did go, they did not display the slightest traces of it afterwards.

I felt deeply the needs of these poor creatures who came every week to my house to get their customary alms. After a time I bought a contribution box, and Christian students of the University of Halle, and other pious people, used to carry it around for me, and sometimes I collected thirty-six cents a week for the benefit of the poor. Still this did not last long; the box used to come in very light, and it seemed as though it hardly paid the trouble of carrying it around. Everybody assured me of their heartiest good wishes, but the poor did not contribute because they *could* not, and the rich did not contribute because they *would* not; and it was painful to see the shifts which some were put to who pretended to be great lovers of the kingdom of God, but who refused to help me and my cause.

Then I took this course: I had a box put up in the sitting-room of my parsonage, with these words painted on it—1 John iii. 17:—"*But whoso hath this world's good, and seeth his brother have need, and shutteth up his bowels of compassion from him, how dwelleth the love of God in him?*" And under that quotation this, 2 Cor. ix. 7:—"*Every man as he purposeth in his heart, so let him give; not grudgingly, or of necessity: for God loveth a cheerful giver.*" Thus every one who came into my house had to *remember* the poor at least, and to open or close the heart against them.

It was in the beginning of 1695 that I put up this box, then I waited a considerable time to see how God would deal with me, and before long I found that I had the Divine blessing.

Sometime before I put up the poor-box in the parsonage, as I was reading the Bible, I came upon these verses. 2 Cor. ix. 8: "*And God is able to make all grace abound toward you; that ye, always having all sufficiency in all things, may abound to every good work.*" These words burned within me. I thought, How can God do it? I would gladly do good to many a poor soul had I the means. But now I must let them go empty handed away, and without any help from me. Some hours after that I received a letter from a Christian friend, who was in the depths of trouble; he was so poor that he and his whole family were threatened with starvation; he would borrow nothing more from any one, and if for the love of God, I would give him something, he would never cease to thank me.

I remembered what I had read just before, and was more troubled than ever to know what to do; I wept and I prayed; and at last I determined, without holding counsel with man, to deal in a Christian way with my friend in his hour of extremity. I carried my purpose into immediate act; and during that year I gave to him a hundred dollars, and rescued his family from the depths of poverty.

This was an excellent proof how God could make me "abound to every good work;" and I cannot omit giving this little instance to show the method in which God has blessed me from the beginning, and heartened me and led me in times of darkness.

About a quarter of a year after I had put up the box in my house, a person dropped in the sum of three dollars and a half. When I came to take it out, and counted it over in my hand (there were seven fifty-cent pieces), I exclaimed with the joy and assurance of faith, "HERE IS A GOODLY CAPITAL TO WORK WITH; I MUST DO A GREAT WORK WITH

THIS ; I WILL FOUND A SCHOOL FOR THE POOR WITH IT."

I took no counsel with flesh and blood, but went on in faith and bought a dollar and a half's worth of books. I then engaged a poor student to instruct the children two hours daily ; I promised to give him eighteen cents a week for his trouble, with full hope that when the crown or two which I had left should be spent, God would open a way to provide me with more.

The beggar children took the books joyfully enough ; but out of the twenty-seven books which were distributed among them, only four ever made their second appearance ; the children sold the others, and then remained away out of shame.

Still I did not allow this to discourage me ; but with the fifty cents which were left I bought more books, which the children always had to leave behind when school was done. After some weeks I made a desk whence the books were always taken in the morning, and where they were laid away at night, as, I believe, is now the custom in all Poor-schools.

At Easter, 1695, this school of mine began with thus slender outfit. For those THREE AND A HALF DOLLARS are the real basis and the first capital on which not only the school for the poor was founded, but from which rose the great Orphan Asylum itself.

II.

THE WORK WIDENS.

I CHOSE for the Poor-school in the summer time a room adjoining my own study, and had a box fastened to the wall, with the inscription, "*For educating poor children, and providing them with the needful books.* Anno MDCXCV." Under the box, I had this verse from Prov. xix. 17, "*He that hath pity upon the poor, lendeth unto the Lord: and that which he hath given, will He pay him again.*"

On Whitsuntide I was visited by some strangers who took a great deal of interest in this new institution, and gave me a few crowns to help on the work, and afterwards some others continued to deposit funds in the box, and thus to encourage my heart and strengthen my hand.

Soon after this, when some of the citizens saw that the poor children were carefully instructed, they wanted to put their children also under the same influences, and so they sent them, and paid three cents a week for their tuition. The teacher was employed five hours daily, and now received fifty cents in addition to the stipend that I paid him.

Alms were distributed to the poor children two or three times weekly to make them love better to come to school, and to help make them more docile and tractable.

Some people out of town heard of what I was doing, and sent trifling sums of money to assist me; others sent parcels of linen to make shirts of, to help sustain the interest of the children in their studies. The school was kept the whole summer through, and the number of pupils, including those who paid their tuition, was between fifty and sixty. In all this it was plain that the blessing of God rested upon us, for there was not a crown collected as capital which He did not Himself give.

I then began to receive the children of noblemen and of wealthy persons, giving them not only special instructors, but also a home with me. This was the beginning of the gymnasium. The occasion for my doing so was that some persons of influence applied to me for students to be private tutors in their families. As I could not respond to their wishes in this matter, because the students most fitted for this duty wished to continue their studies longer in Halle, I advised them to send their children to me, and promised to supply them with suitable teachers; a few were brought at once; others followed as soon as the arrangement was made public.

In the summer of 1695, I received a letter from an influential Christian, in which he offered me, to my entire surprise, three hundred and seventy-five dollars, requesting me to use it entirely at my discretion, for the benefit of poor students. The money arrived soon after, and I saw in it the evident blessing of God upon my work, and felt greatly encouraged to continue in it. This was the first large sum I had received.

This put into my hands ample means for the present. I soon looked up those students who seemed to be in the greatest need, and gave to them various sums—to some twelve cents, to some twenty-five cents, to others thirty-six cents weekly, according to their several necessities—and many a poor student could live here, and prosecute his studies, who never would have been able to have made ends meet without this help, and must have left the University: some indeed had nothing at all, excepting what I gave them. The number whom I assisted in this way was over twenty, the most of them receiving about twenty-four cents weekly.

And this is the beginning of the flowing of that fountain which has never ceased to bless poor students at Halle from that time to this. The Lord's name be praised for it.

The same summer another Christian in high position sent me seventy-five dollars for the benefit of our poor people; and a good friend sent me also fifteen dollars towards maintaining the Poor-school. God showed us in these ways that He would not give up what He had once begun, but would pour down his blessings upon us, and do for us "more than we could ask or even think."

Towards autumn I found it necessary to procure a room for my Poor-school. And since I had no more available space in my own house, I hired a room of my next-door neighbour. The number of the children still increased so much that at the beginning of winter I was compelled to hire even another room. I then divided the pupils, and put the children of citizens under one teacher, and the children of poor parents under another. Each teacher gave instruction four hours daily, and received fifty cents a week besides his board and fuel.

III.

A HOUSE NEEDED.

BUT I soon discovered one fatal defect in my work. Children whom one would reasonably expect to benefit, received little or no advantage. Out of school they lost what little good they gained in school, and then I made the resolution to take some children wholly under my charge, and subject them to constant supervision. *And that was the first call for the building of an Orphan House; that, the first thought which led to the great institution in Halle, conceived before I had the first pound of capital to accomplish the work.*

When I proposed my plan to some few

friends, a spirit of interest was awakened, and three hundred and seventy-five dollars subscribed at once—the interest upon which, twenty dollars, I was allowed to use towards helping on my end.

Seeing the blessing of God upon this measure, I tried to find a poor orphan to educate with the interest of this money. Four poor fatherless and motherless children were brought at once to me, from whom to select one. Relying upon the Lord, I ventured to take all four. Yet as one was taken from my hands, by a family which I trusted, I took the other three; but almost immediately another one came in the place of the one who had been taken. I carried the four to Christian families, and gave thirty-seven cents a week for the care of each child. This was in the autumn of 1695.

I now learned that when one is relying entirely upon God's providence, it is just as safe giving a sovereign as a crown-piece to the poor. For when trusting wholly to God, I ventured to take these four poor orphans, being without the means to provide a home and clothing for scarcely one of them (for the interest of three hundred and seventy-five dollars could hardly do this), I had committed myself unreservedly to God, and relied wholly upon the promise, "the Lord will provide."

So the Orphan House of Halle was begun without reference at all to capital on hand, or to the promise of wealthy people to continue what had been begun, but solely in reliance on the providence of the living God.

The day after I had taken the four orphans spoken of above, two more were brought to me; the next day, another; two days after, another; and a week after, still another: so that by the 16th of November, nine were upon my hands, to be brought up in different Christian families.

I engaged a student of theology, George Henry Neubauer by name, to take a general supervision of them, to provide all that they needed, and to see that they lacked nothing which could contribute to their best welfare, and so these poor children were committed to me before a house was bought or hired, under whose roof they could lie down and sleep.

Meanwhile, the faithful God and Father of the orphan, who can do for us altogether more than we ask or can even think, provided for me more richly than with my faithless reason, I should ever have dared to dream. For He inclined the heart of him who had already given me the three hundred and seventy-five dollars to give me seven hundred and fifty additional at the beginning of the winter.

And in the middle of the winter, another Christian of ample means sent me two hundred dollars to help me in my work, another gave me seventy-five dollars, not so speak of smaller sums, which came in in addition.

And now, by the favour of God, I could not only do something to help poor students gain their education, give a home and clothes to the poor orphans committed to me, and keep in good trim the Poor-school, but I was able to buy the house of my neighbour, of whom I had hired two rooms before, for about three hundred dollars; and in the spring of 1696, I built two apartments in the rear.

The work had been begun in faith, and in faith I meant to continue it, not hesitating to provide all that was needed for the children of my charge, but at the same time guarding against procuring anything not demanded by the sternest necessity.

At the time of my purchasing the adjoining house, and building the two rooms on, as just spoken of, I did not think of appropriating them to the use of the orphans, now twelve in number, yet I determined afterwards to gather them all together from the different families where they were now cared for, and have them all together under one roof. I constituted the student mentioned before the general superintendent of the infant asylum, gave him power to procure beds and bedding, to provide food and drink, to arrange for suitable instruction, and to look after the orderly conduct and the cleanliness of all the orphans; in one word, to assume the duties of a father of twelve children. The removing into the newly-purchased house, however, gave such dignity to the affair, and caused the report of what I was doing to spread to such a degree, that within seven weeks I had eighteen orphans placed under my charge. My house was filled to its utmost capacity, and the duties of the general superintendent became so onerous that I was compelled to engage another man to attend exclusively to the domestic affairs of the household.

IV.

STUDENTS HELPED.

MEANTIME I had appointed an hour every week for the poor students whom I helped, to meet me and receive their allowance. This gave me a good occasion to inquire into their lives and their faithfulness in study, and to form a judgment whether they made a good use of the funds which I committed to them: for with men so young it was difficult to prevent a part of this fund being squandered on useless objects. I resolved, therefore, in God's name, to give out money no longer to the poor students, but to provide them with a free table, relying on that providence to which I trusted implicitly, to make my way clear of pecuniary straits in so doing. I thought that there would be a threefold gain in this course, the money spent in this way would go further than it could in any other way—the provisions being purchased in large quantities at a time. I could have a better opportunity of being with these young men and studying their characters than could be gained in any other way; and those who were not very needy, and spent their weekly allowance in trifles, were freed from that temptation. On the 13th of September, 1696, I ventured on this new experiment in trusting the Lord's goodness. Twenty-four persons sat down to the newly-established free table, including the teachers of the Poor-school, and in this way one thing helped another, for I could provide board for the latter, at less cost in this way than in any other. To accommodate these new demands for space, I first hired and then purchased the house next adjoining the one which I had bought before, and connected them by opening a door between them. They had a common garden, which made this an excellent arrangement.

And all this I may call the founding of the whole institution; the reader has been informed about its feeble beginnings, and its establishment, now I have to portray its growth and enlarged prosperity. I was able now to give alms to the poor, not merely on the Thursdays but every day in the week, and even poor strangers coming from out of town were hospitably entertained, and received our gifts and religious instruction besides.

The Poor-school meanwhile was not neglected. It continued to grow and to demand more accommodation. At the first I had divided it into two classes—one of boys, the other of girls. When these two classes had grown unmanageably large, I divided each of them into two classes according to the age of the scholars. I put over them suitable teachers, and provided them with suitable books; and the movement was so successful that all the poor children in the city who were not able to pay for their schooling were provided by me with all the means for gaining a good education.

The school for the children of townspeople well to do in the world was also continued. In 1697, I made further enlargements, in order to accommodate those who wished to pursue a wider course of studies. I appointed skilful teachers, and formed classes in Latin, Greek, and Hebrew, in history, geography, geometry, music, and botany.

I received fees from such parents as were able to pay for the tuition of their children; but this I may say, because it illustrates my entire trust in Providence, that no one paid me so much as it cost to provide instruction for his child; there was a loss in every case, even where the fees were paid. The very taking of these children of parents of some means increased our own burden, and compelled me to look for even greater blessings from God upon the undertaking.

V.

OUT FROM THE NARROW INTO THE BROAD.

THE number of orphans had so far increased on my hands as to make it necessary to divide them according to sex, giving to each distinct teachers; and as I discovered those that excelled in talents, I selected them out and gave them instructors suited to their greater capacities, providing that they should be taught not only writing and arithmetic, but also the languages and the sciences; while those who were destined to become mechanics and artisans were instructed in the elements of Christianity, as well as in the three R's.

The number of orphans and poor students

who had board gratis, continually increased, and soon the houses which I had purchased became entirely inadequate to our wants. I had to begin to think about a larger house.

Yet there was no model that I could follow; there was no orphan asylum then in all Germany; I could gain no clear idea of the construction and management of other establishments of a similar character in other countries, as there seemed to be no good accounts printed and circulated; I therefore concluded to send George Henry Neubauer, my general superintendent, to Holland, to examine the orphan asylums there, and to make me a report of them, and the method of conducting them, so that nothing which the experience of others could teach me should be wanting to make the orphan asylum at Halle as perfect as any in existence.

As my limitations became still more uncomfortably straitened, I bought the inn known as the "Golden Eagle," standing just outside the Roman gate, for fifteen hundred dollars, and transferred my orphans thither; but I saw very soon that this house was more suitable for a tavern than for my purpose, not to speak of the constant increase of the number of orphans and poor students which soon outgrew even these enlarged accommodations ; for in the spring of this year there were a hundred of the former and seventy-two of the latter; so that with the teachers and servants, there were hard upon two hundred people in the house.

The large open place in front of the "Golden Eagle Inn" was going to be appropriated for a drinking shop and other uses, which I thought not favourable to the interests of the large number of young people committed to my care; I therefore ventured to make a contract for its possession, purposing to proceed to the erection of a house which should be large enough to meet all my needs, for the expense for rent to supply me with the house-room I must have, was not inconsiderable.

And as the whole work had been conducted from the very beginning in entire dependence on the providence of God, and as I had never gone on to take any step with the means in hand for its attainment, but always in the sure expectation that God would open a way, although I had not funds in my possession sufficient to build even a small house, let alone a large one, yet God gave me courage equal to making a fixed resolution that I would go on and build at once.

I summoned Neubauer from Holland, and on the 13th of July, 1698, laid the corner-stone of the Orphan House in the name of God. Providence had blessed me so far that I had on hand a considerable quantity of lumber (though not enough for the edifice); but for other materials and funds to pay workmen, I must look from week to week to the hand of that living God who had already given me such abundant reason to trust Him.

I counted at first on building the whole structure of wood, and the foundation was laid in that expectation, and was therefore light and comparatively unsubstantial; but the architect pronounced the lot of land so suitable to a more substantial edifice, and remonstrated with me so earnestly, and others joined in with him to so great an extent, that I felt almost persuaded to venture deeper, and build in a more stable manner. I soon came unexpectedly into possession of a fine quarry of stone suitable for foundation work, and this seemed another inducement to build of masonry rather than of wood. Yet all this would have been without avail to me unless I had felt able to trust entirely to the providence of God to bless my undertaking.

Although I had begun with no ready money to pay the labourers, yet God opened the way for me to secure, without any difficulty, the services of a sufficient number of workmen to go on with the house. It was my custom, and one to which they yielded a ready compliance, to commence the day, and to end the week, with prayer. And God showed his special care for the undertaking in protecting all the workmen from every serious danger, and in granting speedy recovery to those who were slightly injured during the progress of the building.

Meantime the work advanced so rapidly, despite its magnitude, and the size of the lot of land, together with the hardness of the soil to be removed for the cellar, that in one year from the day when the corner-stone was laid, the roof had covered the whole, and God had silenced the sneers of those who had made light of the whole undertaking, and who had gone so far as to blasphemously say that they would hang themselves on the walls when they should be high enough. At Easter, 1700, the orphans and the students began to take their meals in the new building; very soon all the rooms of the lower storey were completed, and by Easter, 1701, the rooms of the upper storeys were ready for occupation. The King of Prussia showed his appreciation of the work by giving a hundred thousand bricks for the walls, and thirty thousand tiles for the roof, which was a great help to me, and won my heartiest gratitude. The King also granted me the Royal license, and by Act of Incorporation raised the Orphan House to the rank of an institution recognized by the Government.

And now God, who had done all this for the benefit of poor and unfriended orphans, and had become a father to them, inclined the heart of a prominent Christian gentleman to devote a portion of his wealth to found a home for poor widows, and to place it under my care. So I bought a house just outside of Halle, and fitted it up for the accommodation of four widows, a servant and steward, and soon after opened it to this limited number. My means allowed me to provide them with all that was absolutely necessary for life, and to give them about thirty-six cents a week for pocket-money, besides all that they might earn by sewing and spinning. In case of sickness they were provided with medicine and a doctor. Prayers were held with them every day, conducted by the steward of their home ; and we have reason to think that the influence of this widows' retreat was very great, and that their prayers redounded to the benefit of the whole city, as well as the institutions which I had under my charge.

VI.

STRIKING INSTANCES OF GOD'S PROVIDENCE IN DELIVERING ME FROM PECUNIARY EMBARRASSMENTS WHILE GOING ON WITH THE WORK.

I HAVE already given a number of examples to show how graciously and manifestly God anticipated every want, and always made my way ready for me while I knew it not; yet those instances were in reality so striking as well as numerous, that I will speak more at length of them, and recount them.

I do not need, however, to dwell on the general principle of faith in a living God, which was my starting-point of action. Beginning without any other capital than this, and continuing without any other than this, strengthened every step of my way in this belief, I went on not only receiving orphans and poor students under my charge, but venturing on the building of my Orphan House. It must be seen at a glance that a proceeding so unusual must be interesting to trace step by step; that the usual receipts and expenditure would not come and go in the usual fashion; that the novelty of the undertaking would bring much doubt and, perhaps, despondency, or, if entirely successful, much quickening of faith.

The following instances will make all this clear:—

Before the Easter of 1696 came, I was reduced to unusual straits, hardly knowing what we should do the next week. I had not yet become accustomed to be so tightly pressed; but God opened a way at just the right hour, for precisely at the moment of my sorest need, some one (I know not to this day whom, whether man or woman, old or young) was moved to send me seven hundred and fifty dollars. The Lord repay that opportune giver!

At another time we were reduced almost to destitution, and the steward came to me with the tidings that he was out of meat, and grain, and wool, and clothing; I made it at once the subject of special prayer. A person, not of wealth, but of influence, providentially present, became aware of our need, and letting our trying circumstances be known to others, we were at once relieved, and our wants supplied. God asserted the truth of his Word, that He hears the young raven's cry. Directly after my prayer for help in our distress, while I was taking my dinner, some one knocked at my door. I opened it, and found an old friend, who offered me seven pounds. Three more followed thereafter; and so all my wants were supplied, and God showed Himself true to us.

In 1698, a Christian lady sent me a ducat [about two dollars and a quarter], with this word, that once a ducat had come to her most opportunely for her wants, and that she sent me one with the hope and prayer that *God would bless my poor orphans by putting into my hands a great pile of ducats.*

Very soon after, another friend brought me twenty-five ducats more. The same day a person in Sweden sent me two ducats; and not long after, I received through the post twenty-five more, without the donor's name. Not many days elapsed before an old friend of the institution, who had given me money before, sent twenty ducats; and not long after all this, Prince Louis of Würtemburg died, and in his last hours drew from his drawer a satin purse containing five hundred ducats, and said, "This is for the Orphan House at Halle." This last gift was of inestimable service in enabling me to go on with the building.

When this heap of ducats lay before me on the table, I remembered the prayer of the pious lady who sent me the single ducat, and wrote that she hoped that God would send me a great pile of ducats for my orphans.

In February, 1699, I experienced again the most trying want. It was the severe proving of my faith. The larder was destitute, and I knew not which way to turn. I kept revolving over in my mind continually this verse, "Seek ye *first* the kingdom of God and his righteousness, and all other things shall be added unto you;" yet the care of the temporal was constantly wrestling in my soul with my care for the eternal. I had a great effort to cherish my faith in God undisturbed by the want of the present time. As I paid out the last piece of money, I uttered in my heart this prayer, "Domine, respice ad indigentiam meam!" that is, "Lord, look in compassion on my need."

I went forth from my chamber at once, on my way to the University, to deliver my usual lecture to my class, and unexpectedly found a student below, who handed me a package containing seventy dollars, which a friend more than two hundred miles away had sent me for the use of the Orphan House.

And so it always was, that although no half

week went by without bringing heavy demands on me, yet God always anticipated me, and raised up means at the most opportune moment to meet my necessities, and at the same time to strengthen my faith. Gradually I grew strong and untroubled in the conviction that each hour would bring the help to bear its burden, and my faith could not be shaken that God would carry me through, and grant me to see the fulfilment of all my plans and hopes.

On the 10th of March I was wholly out of funds. To my surprise a public hangman came in to see me, and brought me four dollars, which, coming from such a quarter, gave me new assurance of the favour of God.

Soon after this we were out of everything. The steward came in with his accounts, and showed me how sore was our need. I had no money for him, and he had nothing for the household. It was another of our dark hours. I bade him hope on, and have faith, and then continued my own labour (I was dictating), till I had finished what I was on, and then retired to pray. But just as I was closing the door to my room, a merchant appeared, and placed in my hand a roll containing twelve hundred and fifty dollars, to be appropriated to the needs of the Orphan House. I thought of the words of Holy Writ (Isa. lxv. 24), "Before they call, I will answer; and while they are yet speaking, I will hear." Going into my chamber, I offered a prayer of thanksgiving instead of supplication, for my wish and expectation had been changed into perfect fulfilment.

On the 21st of March, I received a letter from the post, enclosing four ducats and this rude couplet:—

"One raised from sickness by the Lord,
Gives this God's goodness to record."

I do not know whence it came, but it was most opportune, for we were entirely without funds.

About Michaelmas we were again reduced to great need; but the weather was so fine and invigorating that it gladdened my heart, and I felt like even exclaiming, How good it is to have nothing, and to rest entirely on God and his constant providence! I was entirely confident that a way would be opened to us out from our place of need, and felt perfect repose in my spirit. The master-mason who had come once before to inquire whether I had any money to pay off the workmen with, came again and asked, "Is anything come yet?" I answered, "No, but I have faith in God." Scarcely had I said the word when a student came to me with thirty dollars in his hand, which he said came from a donor who wished his name to remain unknown. I went at once to the master-workman, and asked him how much money he needed to pay off the men. He answered, "Thirty dollars." "Have you no need of more?" I asked. "No." I told him then how wonderfully God had remem bered us, providing just the sum needed; and the incident served for the strengthening of his faith as well as mine.

Not long after, when I hardly knew which way to turn in order to go on with the building,

I received through the post four hundred dollars with a note from a student stating that that sum had been given him for the use of the Orphan House. I cannot tell how much this confirmed my belief in the kind Providence that was leading us through darkness to light.

One day we were in such want that I repeated with unwonted earnestness the petition, "Give us this day our daily bread." Then I quietly and trustfully waited, being sure that help would presently come. And true enough, my prayer had not long been uttered when a well-known friend rapped at the door and put into my hand four hundred dollars. My earnest prayer was answered.

In the year 1700 I was sick for eight weeks. At last I was able to walk out, and to thank God for permitting me to enjoy again the blessings of light, and air, and exercise, and society, and work; on my walk a paper was given me, and another on my return, each being a cheque for a hundred dollars, and with the second one a letter of great kindness and encouragement, bidding me God-speed in my work. This letter and cheque were from a merchant residing more than five hundred miles away.

At another time a Christian nobleman was visiting me, and inspecting the institution; he saw with pain how narrow were our circumstances, but unfortunately he was himself poor, and unable to assist us. Yet the same day he met a wealthy friend, described our work, and received from him a gift of fifty dollars for us, which he brought with tears, so rejoiced was he at being able to minister thus unexpectedly to our wants.

At another time of want a merchant who lived eight hundred miles from Halle sent me five pounds, in South Germany currency, asking me to take the trouble of expending it in behalf of the Orphan House. Two other donations of the same amount each, soon followed this.

Another time when we were hard pressed God moved the heart of a pious peasant to bring all the money he could hold in his hands. It was one pound in small change. At another time still, a nobleman brought me all that he could hold in both hands. It was twenty-two dollars.

VII.

SPECIAL PROVIDENCES CONTINUED.

IT has often happened that when friends have been present, and have heard of the wonderful manner in which God had succoured us, they have been disposed to do something for us, some instances of which I will mention.

There was present once a Christian stranger who gave me twenty dollars for the poor, and while he was still with me at dinner, there came a lad who brought me twenty dollars, and a written promise that the same amount should follow every year, if the Lord should give health and strength; the lad would not say, however, who sent him, but asked for a receipt and went away. My guest was so affected by this circumstance that he immediately added fifty dollars to his gift. The promise to give me the twenty dollars yearly, I might add, was literally fulfilled.

Of course, the work on which I was engaged was largely spoken about, and it was often the case that when people heard how wonderfully God had blessed my labours, or read about the Orphan House, they felt constrained to assist me. A nobleman, for instance, after reading about the work devoted twenty dollars yearly to it, and always made his remittance promptly. Once when I took some ducats to a broker to be changed into North German currency, when he learned that it was for the poor and the orphans, he added twenty dollars as his own gift.

It happened once that I was in great need of a hundred dollars, but I did not know which way to turn to get one, let alone a hundred. The steward came to me and told me how destitute the house was. I had nothing for him, and told him to come after dinner. Meanwhile, I betook myself to prayer. In the afternoon he came, but I had nothing for him, and bade him come again in the evening. A friend visited me in the after part of the day, and he and I joined in prayer, yet in spite of the necessities of my position and our urgent needs, I did not feel constrained to ask importunately, but on the other hand, was moved to thanksgiving to God for all his past mercies, not only to me, but to all the saints of old. When this good friend took his leave and I opened the front door, there stood on the one side of the entrance the steward who had come again to know if I had anything for him, and on the other side a gentleman who handed me a purse containing a hundred and fifty dollars contributed in behalf of the Orphan House. What could be clearer to me than that the cause I loved and laboured for was under the direct care of God, the eternal and living God, who not for a moment sleeps, and who still testifies that as He was to our fathers, so He is still to us?

At one time I was in need of thirty dollars

to pay the workmen with. There were then visiting me some strangers, one of whom had formerly promised me ten dollars, and the other, four dollars, but had appeared to have forgotten their promise. Meanwhile, I needed the money sorely, yet I had to send my master-workman empty-handed away, telling him that there stands the Orphan House, and up there in the heavens dwells God, and doubtless He will provide for us. He went back and found the workmen standing together, and waiting for their pay. Unexpectedly a friend came up, and the master-workman told him of the difficulty he was in. He at once lent him fifteen dollars, but before he had fairly counted it out, and made it over, I received a gift of thirty dollars, which met all present needs.

At the end of the very next week, I was in want again, and it so happened that Friday was the day for me to settle my household accounts, and Saturday those of the building, yet there was no money on hand for either. But I felt sure it would all come right, I was confident that God would show me a clear token of his care. I quoted the divine promise, 1 Sam. vii. 12, to the steward, "Hitherto hath the Lord helped us ;" and had no doubting about the end. The next day brought fifty dollars.

Another time our necessities were so urgent that the steward was compelled to sell a silver spoon which had been given to us, and yet not even that met our wants. But just then came in most opportunely, when the steward was almost giving up to despair, a hundred dollars, sixty of which were needed at once. Two or three hours after this I received a letter stating that a friend had ten tons and a half of garden produce on the way for me. When the steward saw this double manifestation of God's care, he felt deeply pained at the wicked faithlessness of his heart, and resolved that he never again would distrust the Lord's readiness to provide.

Oftentimes when we felt ourselves destitute, and no large gift came in, we would find in the box nailed up at the door a thaler or a ducat, or a double-ducat piece, enough for present needs, and to show the watchful care of God.

I cannot and need not go further into detail. Other gifts, some of them hundreds of dollars at a time, I received, and as a general rule just when they were most needed. I have entered fully enough into these things to show how wonderfully God anticipated all our wants, and met us just at the hour of need. I ought to say, however, that these gifts were by no means from the rich alone. That verse of Paul, 2 Cor. viii. 2, was eminently true of some of my benefactors, "The abundance of their joy and their deep poverty abounded unto the riches of their liberality." Those who could not give money gave what they could—tin plates and cups, flax and yarn, linen, caps, hats, and stockings, sometimes complete suits of clothing, corn, peas, meat, fish, books, beer, salt, feather-beds and bedding, webs of cloth and remnants, silver forks and spoons, gold rings, costly stones and jewellery of all sorts; in one word, gifts of all kinds and degrees of value, all useful in their way, or capable of being converted into money, and all testifying that a watchful untiring God and a loving Father had the Orphan House in his faithful keeping; that its interests were always dear to Him; and that He never despised my prayers, nor disregarded my faith in his constant providence.

It would be delightful, of course, for me to enter into a detailed summary of all the gifts to us, and the touching and cheering words which have often accompanied them. Since the time of our sore money trials were over, hardly a day has passed without bringing in a donation, either large or small. Ministers struggling to live on narrow incomes have sent us a few shillings, or a pound, or ten, or twenty, or fifty; pious students in the University, out of their meagre funds, have straitened themselves to help us. Widows, not a few, have sent their gifts, and with them their prayers; children have sacrificed the pennies which they had laid by for playthings and sweetmeats, that the orphan children might have a home. I have even had one little gift of a penny where I knew that poverty in its most trying form made even *that* a sacrifice, and it was more to my heart than many dollars would have been from the rich. Nor have these donations been from Germany alone, but from Poland, Sweden, Denmark, Russia, France, England, and, in fact, from almost all the countries of Christendom I have received them. Indeed, from England I have had some of my largest gifts. The entire record (and I have kept it entire) of all the moneys, the articles of jewellery, silver plate, precious stones, clothing, food, and presents, either to be used or to be sold for the benefit of the institution, would fill a volume of much larger size than this. I am amazed as I look back and read page upon page of such records as these :—

From a poor student, three dollars.

From an Austrian merchant, fifty dollars.

From a farmer a little way out of Halle, three tons of vegetables.

From a Christian mother, a diamond ring, which I sold for a hundred and fifty dollars.

From a widow, ten dollars, with a reminder of the promise attending the widow's mite.

From another widow, twenty cents.

From a Bavarian nobleman, twenty dollars, with a promise to pay the same amount yearly during his life.

From a merchant, the bequest of a thousand dollars.

From a little child, with its love and its prayers, nine cents.

From an Englishman, twenty dollars.

From a pastor, thirty-six cents.

From a schoolmaster, fifty cents.

Page after page of such entries I could transcribe, the sums ranging all the way from a few pence up to thousands of dollars. They are repetitions, it is true, one of another, with a slight change of names and amounts, but the effect on the mind, on seeing the stupendous columns, and the immense aggregates, makes one cry out, "What hath God wrought!" In the letters accompanying these gifts, all the sweet Bible words about faith in God, all the gracious promises of God were revealed, and used to fill my heart with joy. But it would defeat my purpose to reproduce them all here. Enough has been given already to show how graciously God led us, how hard He tried us at first, how widely He opened his hand afterwards, when we had "proved Him," and showed us that indeed He had a blessing for us too large to receive.

VIII.

THE ACT OF INCORPORATION. SICKNESS IN THE HOUSE.

IN 1698 the Prussian Government recognized my work and its public utility, by giving me a regular act of incorporation, and by allowing me to solicit contributions in all parts of the kingdom. This my friends considered a great step gained, and I do not wish to say that it may not have been to my advantage, for doubtless it was in accordance with the wise though hidden purpose of God, but the consequences which followed it were, judging by human appearances alone, far from beneficial to my undertaking.

One thing which stood in my way was the cost of collecting contributions. But when you consider the difficulty and expense of procuring a small army of collectors of the right stamp, men both capable and trustworthy, you will see that only in the shrewdest manner could the bare cost of collecting be met, not to speak of accumulating a great sum for an object so little known and understood as mine. For the Orphan House in Halle was the first one of the kind in Germany; the public mind was not prepared to admit its claims unchallenged, and it was a great work to get a hearing. The end was, that only in Berlin and in three provinces did I make any attempt at taking contributions, and there with but meagre success.

But other evils came in. It was commonly supposed that because the Government had recognized the institution, it had largely endowed it, and would provide amply for all its wants. Those who had known of my trials supposed them at an end, and felicitated me on my good fortune and the happy issue of those wearisome years of poverty and uncertainty. Those who had been donors before, now ceased to give, for they saw no necessity longer of individual contributions, now that the State had taken the Orphan House in charge; and not only so, but they felt free to send us any number of poor and homeless children, supposing that our endowment was ample enough to meet any exigency. It was even reported that I was in the receipt of twelve thousand dollars yearly from the Prussian Government! No wonder that I was overrun with applications! Between the neglect of friends on the one hand, in the fancied idea of my liberal allowance from the King, and the crowds of applicants on the other, I was worse off than I had ever been. I should have been glad to go back to the old ways. In fact, I found the principle of dependence on faith and prayer the best. While I relied on God I was successful, but when I began to felicitate myself on gaining a strong arm of flesh, I began to see my weakness. After all, the way in which I began asserted itself as more reliable in all its contingencies and exigencies than the help of an earthly king, however kindly disposed and strong.

One of the sorest evils we had to contend with, in consequence of the crowded state of the House, was sickness. We were remarkably favoured indeed, in receiving without expense the services of an eminent physician of Leipsic in assisting our own house-doctor in difficult cases, yet the rooms were so full that it made it very difficult to care properly for the sick. Added to this was the fact that the year 1699 was signalized by the prevalence of a peculiarly malignant type of fever which seized on the most vigorous and blooming, sparing the weak and ill-conditioned. We contended with it in vain. It seized upon the teachers as well as the taught, and hurried them into a common grave. No medicine then known seemed to have any power to stay its course : it yielded to no treatment. We knew not which way to turn to stop its ravages, but I bethought me of the power of prayer, and God graciously heard me ; and not long after, a physician in another place sent me a specific, which proved efficacious in saving life and in averting the disease. And I am sure that it will not be thought fanciful that God should be able to stay the progress of disease, by blessing the use of natural agents, and by directing the attention to them. He does not arrest sickness by naked power, but He is abundantly able to incline the hearts of skilful physicians to serve the poor, and He is not less able to direct the mind than the heart, and can easily open human eyes to the hidden uses of nature in healing diseases.

I will not close this chapter without acknowledging the kindness and true Christian spirit of all the people who have approached me claiming to be friends of the enterprise. It might be supposed that some might be drawn to me in hope of pecuniary advantage or selfish aims, but I have never found traces of that spirit; a lofty disinterestedness has always been the most striking characteristic of those with whom I have had dealings. It would be pleasant to speak in detail of benefactors of the House, but I cannot do so; and in fact one wonderful feature of all the Lord's conduct of this matter has been that the names of the donors have been unknown to me even to this time. This hints at the true undertone of the whole; that the springs were indeed moved of God; that men gave "as they were moved of the Holy Ghost." Hardly a great gift came accompanied with the name of the donor; that was withheld out of a modesty which I did not always understand, but now know to have been indicative of the need that God should have all the glory.

IX.

GREATER DIFFICULTIES THAN THE WANT OF MONEY: TRIUMPHANT DELIVERANCE.

IT must be thought by my reader that pecuniary difficulties were the only ones that I had to contend with; there were others that were more trying to my feelings than even the narrow circumstances to which I was subjected. True, it was a daily trial of faith to rely implicitly on the care of Providence; those who have a full purse know that it is no slight thing to provide for the wants of some hundreds of persons; but with nothing in the larder, and with nothing in the purse, it needs no imagination to see that one must be hard pressed oftentimes to know which way to turn; and that I often was, for it did not always happen that God met my wants *just* at the hour of need; sometimes I was compelled to cry out with the Psalmist, "How long, O God, how long?"—and I have known the time when, for want of money to buy a few candles, we have all spent a whole evening in darkness, and been brought to pretty sharp hunger.

But harder to bear than this were the misapprehensions of people who tried to work upon the public mind, and prejudiced it against me. All kinds of charges were made; and those opposed to religion were influenced to believe that I was an impostor or a fanatic. Those were provings of my spirit more subtle and powerful than any others I ever met. It was said that it was madness to build on so huge a scale. What could a vast system of houses be for? Why not confine myself to the accommodations with which I begun? I made brief answer to this—"That the Lord was rich enough to pay for it all; that I had not gone to work without counting the cost, for I knew that the Great Steward of the universe would think the paying the expenses of the Orphan House at Halle a very little thing."

It was said that I abused the children; that I gave them food which swine ought not to eat, and meagre at that. Such idle reports I could not meet in palpable shape, and disprove them; but they died at last as all lies will. Yet it was sore to bear this; for though we were at times pinched for food, yet it was very seldom. My pecuniary embarrassments were more generally in the way of my going on with the building than with the common wants of the body, and there was never any protracted suffering. There was such system in the whole direction that I knew just how everything was managed; and I knew that the table was always wholesome and abundant enough.

It was alleged that large sums of money came into my hands, which I appropriated to my private use; that I was laying up riches for my family to enjoy after my death; and as this stung as a poisoned arrow, it needed faith—a great deal of faith in God—to go on my way amid such charges as this; but God bade me look up and go on. The rumours of great amounts of money lying in my hands drew crowds of orphans and indigent persons to my door—far more than I had any accommodations for, spacious as were the new buildings. It was said that I had one room *full* of money—gifts of ten thousand dollars were spoken of as of not unfrequent occurrence; and it was reported that my great trouble was to know what to do with it all. Meantime the public never saw into the real state of the case. During all the time, when hundreds were thronging in, I was never a day without being more or less straitened; large and frequent as were the donations, after the work was fairly under weigh, yet they never surpassed our urgent needs, and while crowds were standing in the outer hall, some living at a great distance from Halle, and *demanding* help, my steward would sometimes be in close consultation how we could give our own orphans a dinner. Thus wrongly was I misjudged, and evil spoken of. It was also said that I was becoming secular in my habits; that having become a business man I had lost all my pious habits; that I was engrossed in money affairs, and could not be expected to attend to religion at the same time. God forgive those my accusers, and give them more of what they missed in me!

They said also that I neglected my pastoral office, for it will not be forgotten that all this time I was a pastor, and had my own church to care for; and it is true that the great and growing interests of the Orphan House drew me away from the duties of my pastorate; but I saw that my place was made good by a man of great excellence and worth; and not till then did I feel that I could accept the new trusts that God had plainly assigned me. I remained the nominal pastor, and as far as I could I supervised the spiritual interests of my church; but the adjunct pastor assumed the most of the active labours of the position.

But it would be in vain for me to recount all the false and wicked charges which were brought against me. Happily God strengthened me, so that I went on despite them all. The openly irreligious people made light, of course, of an undertaking that rested on prayer and faith as its basis, and it grieved me to see their unconcealed opposition. But worse than theirs was the faithlessness of cold-hearted nominal believers—men who pretended to trust God, but who could not take Him at his promise. But the end justified all my confidence, and shamed their unbelief. I had not reckoned, the result proved, without my host. I became "more than conqueror through Him that loved us and died for us." And the Orphan House at Halle, with its ample appointments and its flourishing dependencies, stands as the visible monument of the wonderful favour of God.

The favour of the Prussian Government has been displayed to me in a remarkable degree, and the favour of good men, not in my own country alone, but throughout all Christendom. The institution is at the time that I write put on such a foundation that, humanly speaking, and as far as can be seen now, it will be a perpetual blessing to Germany and the world. Its funds are ample, and its management has, I have every assurance, the public confidence. For all this I desire now, and while I live, to bless the Lord. He was my counsellor from the beginning, and my leader all through the work, and to Him and Him alone be all the glory.

X.

THE RESULT,

AS stated in a letter by Baron Canstein,* in 1706, to a member of the Prussian Government:—

"MY DEAR SIR,—I have recently visited the great establishment at Halle, which was founded and has been brought to its present advanced prosperity by Professor Francke, of the University in that city. My visit was so pleasant

* The writer of this letter was later the founder of the Canstein Bible Society, an institution which publishes its works at Francke's Orphan House, and sends them forth from there. It has been a great blessing to Germany, and is still in active operation.

and so quickening to my faith, that I cannot deny myself the privilege of describing the institution, as it exists now—a kind of little world, yet all in harmony and a state of great efficiency. The history of the rise of this Home for Orphans, with its dependent schools, is not a common one; it is not the common-place development of an institution which has been fostered by Government patronage, but it is one that began in FAITH, and has been continued in faith up to the present time. Relying on the great fact that God IS, that He still 'moves,' as well as 'has his being,' Professor Francke has been emboldened to go on with this work, beginning it without capital, and only expecting that God would provide from day to day. He had dared to build a system of edifices of palatial size, believing that God would dispose the hearts of his children to give the necessary means; and he has been justified in this trust, for the Orphan House is complete, is paid for, and is still in the receipt of means to sustain its usefulness.

"Francke's Institution, as it perhaps ought

strictly to be called, is a unit, by virtue of one controlling purpose—viz., the exercise of a wise charity, and by virtue of the strong, clear mind and will which direct all its movements. Professor A. H. Francke is pastor of the church in Glaucha, a suburb of Halle, and a Professor in the University of Hálle. Yet unit though it is, it unifies many diverse things, and is made up of parts, in themselves very unlike. It is a bundle of sticks which do not resemble one another at all, and yet make a whole of great strength and unity. I will speak of these parts one by one.

"The first is—

"THE DIVINITY SCHOOL,

An institution which grew out of the necessity for helping poor students of theology, and of using their services at the same time as teachers of the destitute children. From the very first, Francke employed indigent young men studying in the University, as his co-labourers in the Orphan House, and in the schools for the poor. Many a young man has been saved to the ministry in consequence of this help; many a wise teacher has been trained by the preparatory drill which he has gained under Francke. Funds came in from the very first to help indigent students, and they now enjoy a free table in the general dining-room of the House, they have apartments for study, and receive special instruction in the ancient languages. Professors in the University come to the Orphan House, and give their lectures on Hebrew, Greek, and Oriental literature: the Hebrew Bible is now printing in the House, under the auspices of the professor in this department; and thus ends so varied are made to help each other; the students are always at hand when they are needed as instructors; the cost of providing their food is a light expense when so many hundreds are to be fed, and the rooms are as commodious as those of the University proper for the purpose of lectures.

"THE TEACHERS' SEMINARY.

As the Theological Seminary was mainly for the advantage of young men who wished to become clergymen, it was early deemed good to found a department where thorough teachers might be trained. The needs of the orphans and the destitute children were so urgent at the outset, that Francke had to look around to secure help, and none stood so ready at his hand as young men of needy circumstances, who wished to gain an education. Many of these were pious, and exercised a healthful religious influence over the young. He began with only ten, giving them a home with him and a small salary besides, and claiming from three to five hours daily of them as teachers. The increase of the schools, demanded an increase of instructors, and the number expanded gradually to its present size. The studies pursued in the seminary are mainly those which will be of special service in teaching the children, and far more attention is given to a thorough acquaintance with the rudiments, than with branches which will be foreign to their after use. The means for providing all these men with their living, and the stipend which is paid to them, have always come as the response to faith; no man has been asked for it; no provision has been made by Government for it; all has been in answer to the 'fervent effectual prayer of the righteous man.' This department has been a great blessing to the Orphan House, and I might even say to Germany, for the five years' course of instruction secures the most competent instructors for the great schools of the kingdom.

"THE FREE TABLE.

The free table is an excellent feature in Francke's institution, and one which finely illustrates the faith of the founder. It was, humanly speaking, very hazardous for a clergyman without means to open his house to twelve young men, and offer them their board free; but Francke did it, and was justified in it. He believed in God, and it was imputed to him for righteousness; and the Lord opened the hearts of his children, so that in a short time Francke gave their meals to yet twelve more, soon to twelve more, and now the number is almost a hundred of these young men who sit down in the great hall of the Orphan House. This provision secures an ample supply of wholesome food to these young students; for it was found to be the case that many were so self-denying in their efforts to gain an education, that they begrudged themselves an adequate supply of nourishing food. But now they must have it, and besides a dollar is spent to far better advantage when laid out in providing for hundreds than for one. The free table affords also an excellent opportunity for Professor Francke to study the character of the young men. If any are impostors, he finds it out; and they know each other, and are better known than they could be if they lived alone, and boarded themselves. The table, too, is made a means of religious improvement. A chapter of Scripture is read, and remarks are made. A hymn is sung, and a constant effort is made to keep in mind the bountiful hand of God. Nor does this lead to a mechanical, perfunctory service, as it might under other circumstances; but the peculiar history of the institution, and the unquestioned faith of Professor Francke, make every meal a religious enjoyment and a means of grace.

"THE LATIN SCHOOL.

If Francke's institution has any offshoot which is not connected with it by the tie of organic life, it is this. It is a school for the children of the nobility, and of people well to do in the world, who desire instruction in the advanced branches. It took its rise thus:—When Francke was beginning his schools for the poor and for orphans, it was soon found out in Halle and the neighbourhood that he was a man of remarkably sound judgment, energy, Christian character, and skill as an educator. He was earnestly asked to select young men whom he might recommend unqualifiedly as private tutors, and let them go from his humble house to the mansions of the rich. This he did not choose to do. He preferred to keep the young men around him, and have an eye to all their progress.

But he proposed to certain of the nobility to send their sons to live under his roof, and be instructed there; they did so, and the 'Pädagogium,' or Latin School, thus sprung into being—at first embracing but twelve pupils, but now, after a lapse of only about ten years, embracing between fifty and sixty. Here instruction is given in the ancient and modern languages, in all the polite branches of literature, and in the sciences. Yet it would be unfair to pass by the fact, that this institution is not, and has never been, self-supporting. Were it not for the other schools, Professor Francke would not receive enough, even from the rich, to be able to educate their sons. So the Latin School links in with all the rest, and shares a common blessing. The same living and loving God watches over its interests who watches over all the rest. The same Beneficence which preserves the school for orphans, preserves the school for the sons of noblemen. God's hand is extended in blessing over the whole great institution.

"THE ORPHAN HOUSE PROPER.

The fourth department is that of the Orphans, embracing the system of buildings where they are lodged, and have their instruction. The name Orphan House is given, indeed, to the whole congeries of buildings; but it is apparent that the home of the orphans is but a part of Francke's institution. Yet it is the part which most fills the public eye, and draws the public sympathy; and it is to that that Francke has devoted himself with the most assiduous care. The main building devoted to this purpose is six storeys in height, about one hundred and fifty feet wide, and is handsomely finished. It is by far the largest building in the city, and is really imposing in its appearance. There are many military barracks, which only give the observer the idea of size; but the main building of the Orphan House is not only colossal in proportions, but symmetrical, and a great ornament to the city. The whole house is built in the form of a hollow square, and the buildings on three sides of the rectangle are not elegant—simply commodious. It is the large building on the fourth side which attracts the most attention, standing as it does on one of the large public squares of the city. There are buildings adapted to all the varied wants of a large colony of children—a bake-house, a brew-house, a slaughter-house, a gymnasium, a wash-house, together with the dining, sleeping, and school-rooms needed for more than a thousand souls. And all this was built without any accumulation of capital. From day to day the Lord provided what was required, and Francke received, in answer to his prayers, without asking the assistance of any man, every dollar to pay the workmen, and buy all the materials. He began with nothing; he never was beforehand with his means, yet he received so much, that though venturing to build of brick and stone, and in an expensive style of finish, he was not in arrears for this work. It is a signal trial of faith, and it is so regarded by all true Christians. Since the work was done, the same loving Father has continued to supply all the wants of the inmates; and although there have been hours of darkness, yet the Lord has always shown his mercy in the end.

"THE APOTHECARIES' DEPARTMENT.

The frequent cases of sickness in so large a collection of children, early made it necessary to provide for this class of needs. The apothecary department, now of much magnitude, began with the boiling of herbs for tea, and with the preparation of common household medicaments. It now has its large dispensary, with separate rooms for putting up and storing medicines, and is much used by the inhabitants of the city. Some of the remedies which have been employed by the house-physician have proved signally efficacious, and a gentleman in possession of a medicine called by him *essentia dulcis* bequeathed the receipt of its manufacture to Professor Francke. The income from this source is very large (twenty thousand dollars yearly), and the cures which have been wrought by it amazing, and are certified to by the leading regular physicians of the city and neighbourhood. The gift of this gentleman has done much to enrich the institution, and to put it on a permanent foundation.

"THE BOOK-STORE.

Very early Professor Francke provided the children who came under his charge with books, and as the institution has advanced, the need of a department to meet this want became so obvious as to lead to the establishment of a large book-store, where are kept all the works published at the institution, and a general assortment of useful works. This, too, is now large, and meets the wants of a great number of people in the city, who make their purchases at the House rather than elsewhere.

"THE PUBLISHING DEPARTMENT.

There having been expressed a wish that a sermon of Francke's should be widely circulated, a project was started that it be printed in the

House. A press was procured, types and ink bought, a printer hired, and the sermon was published. This was the beginning of the publishing department, which, under the blessing of God, has expanded till it has become one of the first establishments of the kind in Germany. Not long after Francke began to publish, a great impetus was given to the effort by the unexpected proposal of the distinguished Spener, that one of his works should issue from the publishing department of the Orphan House. Thenceforward it became a power in the land; and now, not only are all the school-books used in the institution printed and bound under its own walls, but works in Hebrew and the Oriental languages have appeared, besides standard religious works. The whole management has been conducted with an eye to the good of the Church of Christ; nothing of doubtful character has been allowed to appear, and Francke's wise and careful supervision has been bestowed on every work issued. The founts of types in the Greek, Hebrew, Syriac, and Arabic characters, are among the most complete in the land. Among the works of a learned character issued, may be mentioned Boyle's 'Dissertation on the Style of the Scriptures,' translated into French and German. The binding and printing-house have been self-supporting, as much of the labour is done by the larger lads in the schools."

(The distinguished author of this letter does not refer to the great Bible-publishing department established by himself within the Orphan House, using its presses, binding, etc., and well known to this day as the Canstein Bible Depository, a most valuable means of circulating the Scriptures through Germany. Over five millions of Bibles have been scattered over the country through Baron Canstein's efforts, and there is no cessation in the good work. I may remark that Canstein was the inventor of the art of stereotyping; he first applied it to the Bibles issued by him).—Ed.

"OTHER ELEEMOSYNARY DEPARTMENTS.

Under the broad roof of the Orphan House

are clustered besides all the agencies specified, a home for widows, an establishment for the care of poor people, in Glaucha (the suburb of Halle in which the buildings stand), and an establishment for strolling beggars.

And this great and comprehensive charity has all been carried into effect through the efforts of a single man! Who shall doubt the power of faith? who shall now doubt the power of prayer?"

XI.

CLOSING NOTE BY THE EDITOR.

SINCE the introduction of this little work was written, and the rest of its pages were culled from Francke's voluminous documents and translated, I have been so happy as to pay another visit to this flourishing institution. It still maintains its old reputation, and never was it more influential for good than at the present day. The Director, Dr. Kramer, a brother-in-law of the great geographer, Carl Ritter, is not only eminent for his attainments in Greek literature, but for his efficiency as the manager of a great and complicated system of schools and foundations like this. In the Pädagogium, I had the pleasure of meeting and making the acquaintance of the distinguished geographer, Professor Daniel, the German editor of "Ritter's University Lectures," a man of great urbanity, and of the kindliest presence. But a word of special acknowledgment is due to Dr. Tschischnitz, the English teacher in the institution, who did me the favour to conduct me to every part of the great pile of buildings. Let no visitor to Halle fail to call upon this courteous gentleman, who is quite at home in our language, and who will, I am quite sure, be pleased to act as cicerone. The statue of Francke, executed by the great sculptor, Rauch, stands near the end of the square enclosed by the buildings, and is a most happy conception, portraying the good man with an orphan child grasping each hand. The buildings recently erected, especially the Re-al School, testify to the constant expansion of the institution, and its ability to meet new wants, and the one just referred to might for elegance and convenience be taken as a model in England or America. Nor has the printing department fallen behind, while so much else has been advancing. No greater contrast can be easily conceived than between the reports of Francke which I have used in the preparation of this work, and the books which are published at the Orphan House now: some of them works of great eminence, such as the German edition of Robinson's "Biblical Researches." Indeed, the printing now executed there is so admirable that many English publishing houses carry their books through the Orphan House press. I mention these things to show how faithful God still remains to those who have continued faithful to Him. One cannot go into the great dining-room and see five hundred lads, neatly dressed, light-hearted, well-mannered, come and take their places, while one of their number repeats the familiar German grace—

> "Lord Jesus, come, and be our Guest,
> And let thy blessing on us rest,"

without feeling grateful that Francke lived and made all things ready, so that destitute children almost two hundred years after him, should have all this care, and good nurture.

And thus it is, whatever else may fail, God abides sure. His promises are as durable as the foundations of the earth. Whoever else prove false, God may be trusted. Francke was a simple-hearted, true, believing man; but every man in our time who has the same faith may have the same blessing. For God and Christ are the same, yesterday, to-day, and for ever.

THE END.

HARRILD, PRINTER, LONDON.

SAMPSON LOW AND CO.'S

LIST OF PUBLICATIONS.

A WALK FROM LONDON TO THE LAND'S END.

BY ELIHU BURRITT.

Author of "A Walk from London to John O'Groat's."

With several Illustrations. Large post 8vo. Uniform with the First Edition of "John O'Groats." 12*s*.

A WALK FROM LONDON TO JOHN O'GROAT'S.

With Notes by the Way.

BY ELIHU BURRITT.

Second and Cheaper Edition. With Photographic Portrait of the Author. Small post 8vo. 6*s*.

A THOUSAND MILES IN THE ROB ROY CANOE;

OR, RIVERS AND LAKES OF EUROPE.

BY JOHN MACGREGOR, M.A.

Fourth Edition. With a Map and numerous Illustrations. Fcap. 8vo, cloth. 5*s*.

A SECOND CANOE VOYAGE IN NORWAY, SWEDEN, ETC.

BY JOHN MACGREGOR, M.A.

With a Map and numerous Illustrations. Fcap. 8vo.

DESCRIPTION OF THE NEW ROB ROY CANOE.

BUILT FOR A

VOYAGE THROUGH NORWAY, SWEDEN, AND THE BALTIC.

Dedicated to the Canoe Club by the Captain. With Illustrations. Price 1*s*.

CAPTAIN HALL'S LIFE WITH THE ESQUIMAUX.

New and Cheaper Edition, with Coloured Engravings and upwards of 100 Woodcuts. With a Map. Price 7*s*. 6*d*. cloth extra. Forming the cheapest and most popular edition of a work on Arctic Life and Exploration ever published.

"*This is a very remarkable book, and unless we very much misunderstand both him and his book, the author is one of those men of whom great nations do well to be proud.*"—SPECTATOR.

A WINTER IN ALGERIA, 1863-4.

BY MRS. GEORGE ALBERT ROGERS.

With Illustrations. 8vo, cloth. 12*s*.

THE VICARIOUS SACRIFICE;

GROUNDED ON PRINCIPLES OF UNIVERSAL OBLIGATION.

By HORACE BUSHNELL, D.D., Author of "Nature and the Supernatural," etc.

Crown 8vo. Price 7s. 6*d*.

"*An important contribution to theological literature, whether we regard the amount of thought which it contains, the systematic nature of the treatise, or the practical effect of its teaching. . . . . No one can rise from the study of this book without having his mind enlarged by its profound speculation, his devotion stirred by its piety, and his faith established on a broader basis of thought and knowledge.*"—GUARDIAN.

Also by the same Author.

CHRIST AND HIS SALVATION. 6*s*.
NATURE AND THE SUPERNATURAL. 3*s*. 6*d*.
CHRISTIAN NURTURE. 1*s*. 6*d*.
CHARACTER OF JESUS. 6*d*.
NEW LIFE. 1*s*. 6*d*.
WORK AND PLAY. 3*s*. 6*d*.

THE LAND AND THE BOOK;

OR,

BIBLICAL ILLUSTRATIONS DRAWN FROM THE MANNERS AND CUSTOMS, THE SCENES AND THE SCENERY, OF THE HOLY LAND.

BY W. M. THOMSON, M.D., twenty-five years a Missionary in Syria and Palestine.

With 3 Maps and several hundred Illustrations. 2 vols. Post 8vo, cloth. £1 1*s.*

MISSIONARY GEOGRAPHY FOR THE USE OF TEACHERS AND MISSIONARY COLLECTORS.

Fcap. 8vo, with numerous Maps and Illustrations. 3*s.* 6*d.*

A TOPOGRAPHICAL PICTURE OF ANCIENT JERUSALEM.

Beautifully Coloured. Nine feet by six feet, on rollers, varnished. £3 3*s.*

THE LIGHT OF THE WORLD:

A MOST TRUE RELATION OF A PILGRIMESS TRAVELLING TOWARDS ETERNITY; DIVIDED INTO THREE PARTS, WHICH DESERVE TO BE READ, UNDERSTOOD, AND CONSIDERED BY ALL WHO DESIRE TO BE SAVED.

Reprinted from the Edition of 1696. Beautifully printed by Clay, on Toned Paper. Crown 8vo, pp. 593, bevelled boards. 10*s.* 6*d.*

THE MISSION OF GREAT SUFFERINGS.

BY ELIHU BURRITT.

Crown 8vo.

FAITH'S WORK PERFECTED:

THE RISE AND PROGRESS OF THE ORPHAN HOUSES OF HALLE.

From the German of Francke.

BY WILLIAM L. GAGE.

Fcap.

THE LIFE OF THE LATE DR. MOUNTAIN, BISHOP OF QUEBEC.

8vo, cloth. Price 10*s*. 6*d*.

A SHORT METHOD OF PRAYER;

AN ANALYSIS OF A WORK SO ENTITLED BY MADAME DE LA MOTHE GUYON.

'BY THOMAS C. UPHAM,
Professor of Mental and Moral Philosophy in Bowdoin College, U.S., America.

Printed by Whittingham. 12mo, cloth. 1s.

CHRISTIAN BELIEVING AND LIVING.

BY F. D. HUNTINGTON, D.D.

Crown 8vo, cloth. 3*s*. 6*d*.

LIFE THOUGHTS.

BY THE REV. HENRY WARD BEECHER.

Two Series, complete in one volume, well printed and well bound. 2*s*. 6d. Superior Edition, illustrated with ornamental borders. Sm. 4to, cloth extra. 7*s*. 6*d*.

DR. BEECHER'S LIFE AND CORRESPONDENCE: AN AUTOBIOGRAPHY.

EDITED BY HIS SON.

2 vols, post 8vo, with Illustrations. Price 21*s*.

LIFE AND EXPERIENCE OF MADAME DE LA MOTHE GUYON.

BY PROFESSOR UPHAM.

Edited by an English Clergyman.

Crown 8vo, cloth, with Portrait. Third Edition. 7*s*. 6*d*.

By the same Author.

LIFE OF MADAME CATHERINA ADORNA. 12mo, cloth. 4*s*. 6*d*.
THE LIFE OF FAITH, AND INTERIOR LIFE. 2 vols. 5*s*. 6*d*. each.
THE DIVINE UNION. 7*s*. 6*d*.

www.ingramcontent.com/pod-product-compliance
Lightning Source LLC
LaVergne TN
LVHW021425110826
845150LV00007B/2085

* 9 7 8 1 4 2 5 5 0 8 3 4 0 *